Let's Read with Alex and Steve

Level 2

Written by
Rita Lott

Pixel Page Press

Illustrated by
Elvis Tapley

BOSS MODE!

_____

can read this book!

For ZJC-

We can conquer any mob together.

-RL

Copyright © 2024 by Dovetail Readers

Pixel Page Press is an imprint of Dovetail Readers.

All rights reserved.

No part of this publication may be reproduced, distributed, or transmitted in any form or by any means, including photocopying, recording, or other electronic or mechanical methods, without the prior written permission of the publisher, except as permitted by U.S. copyright law. For permission requests, contact the author at pixelpagepress.com.

The story, all names, characters, and incidents portrayed in this production are fictitious. No identification with actual persons (living or deceased), places, buildings, and products is intended or should be inferred.

NOT AN OFFICIAL MINECRAFT PRODUCT.

NOT APPROVED BY OR ASSOCIATED WITH MOJANG.

Table of Contents

Let's Review 3

Buzz Off! 6

Steve Is Stuck 22

Boss Mob 36

Hiss! 52

Let's Level Up! 70

Scope and Sequence 72

How To Use This Book

Sound out these words.

 Learn these words by heart.

Earn Experience Points (XP) to level up!

Visit pixelpagepress.com for more information about what your Minecraft reader is learning in each book.

Let's earn XP!

The XP bar fills up with each challenge you complete!

LET'S REVIEW!
Solve the riddle to earn 10XP

Help Steve dig down to the bottom.
Read the clues and write the words.
Only one letter changes each time!

___ ___ ___

Very warm

___ ___ ___

Something you wear on your head

___ ___ ___

A flying animal that sleeps upside down

___ ___ ___

An animal that says "meow"

___ ___ ___ ___

Many animals that say "meow"

Read this story to earn

10XP

Buzz Off!

Story 1

Read these words to earn

5XP

| buzz | lick | hill | back |

down her look

then she

honey

Phonics Focus: double consonants, -ck

Alex is sad.

The pot has no honey in it.

Alex licks her lips. She packs the pot in her bag.

Alex sets off up the hill.

But then . . .

Alex looks down. Yuck!

She has ticks

on her socks!

"Buzz off!" Alex yells.

She picks the ticks off.

But then . . .

Alex looks down. Yuck!

A bug sucks on her leg!

"Buzz off!" Alex yells.

She kicks the bug off.

Alex looks up.

She sees a log.

It has moss on it.

Alex gets down.

She looks in the log.

Yes! Lots of honey!

She fills up the pot.

But then . . .

BUZZ!

BUZZ!

BUZZ!

Alex runs!
She runs back down the hill.

Alex has got a lot of honey in her pot.

The End

Answer these questions to earn 5XP

1. What did Alex see on her socks? Find the WORD that answers the question.

2. What did Alex do when she saw a bug on her leg? Find the SENTENCE that answers the question.

3. Why did Alex look in the log?

4. What did Alex mean when she told the bees to buzz off?

5. Can you think of a more polite way someone could ask to be left alone?

Read this story to earn

10XP

Steve Is Stuck!

Story 2

Read these words to earn

5XP

Phonics Focus: blends, multisyllabic words

Steve likes to swim.

He jumps off the dock.

Steve swims and swims.
He spots a clam
and a crab.

But then . . .
Steve swims
into the kelp.
Steve gets stuck!

Steve kicks his legs.

He kicks and kicks.

But Steve cannot get the kelp off.

He cannot swim up to the top.

Steve yells to Crab.

Can Crab help him?

Yes, Crab can help!

Crab snips the kelp.

He gets Steve unstuck!

SNIP!

Steve swims for the top.

POP!

Steve is glad to be back on the dock!

The End

Answer these questions to earn 5XP

1. Where did Steve get stuck? Find the WORD that answers the question.

2. What did Crab do to help Steve? Find the SENTENCE that answers the question.

3. How did the bubbles change while Steve was underwater?

4. First, Steve got <u>stuck</u>. Then he got <u>unstuck</u>. How are these words the same and different?

5. Do you like to swim? How do you stay safe in the water?

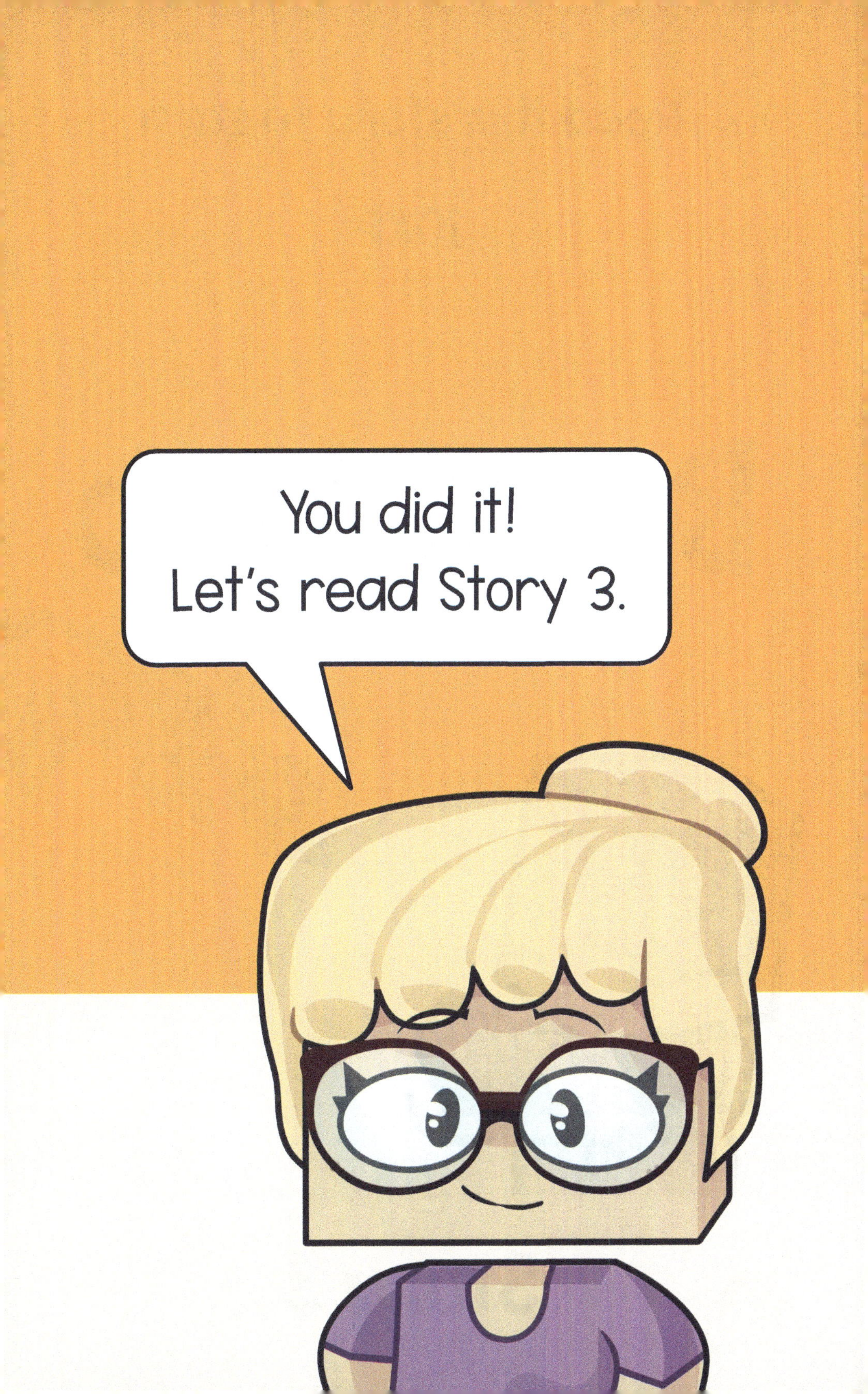
You did it!
Let's read Story 3.

Read this story to earn

10XP

Boss Mob

Story 3

Read these words to earn

5XP

- boss
- snack
- egg
- hunt

- we
- are

A "boss mob" is a special creature that is very hard to defeat. In Minecraft, you must beat the Ender Dragon to win the game!

Phonics Focus: Blends practice

Steve and Alex are on the hunt for a snack.

39

Steve looks down.

He spots an egg.

We can snack on this egg!

But Alex looks up.

She yells to Steve.

Steve looks up.

It is a dragon!

Gasp!
A boss mob!

The dragon is mad.

It flaps at Steve.

"Alex, I will toss the egg to you!" Steve yells.

Alex grabs the egg.
Steve tells Alex to run.

But Alex just looks
at the egg.
She looks back
at the dragon.

This egg is not a snack.

Alex sets the egg
in the soft grass.
The dragon grabs
the egg and flaps off.

Steve and Alex grin big grins.

It was a big boss mob.

No . . .

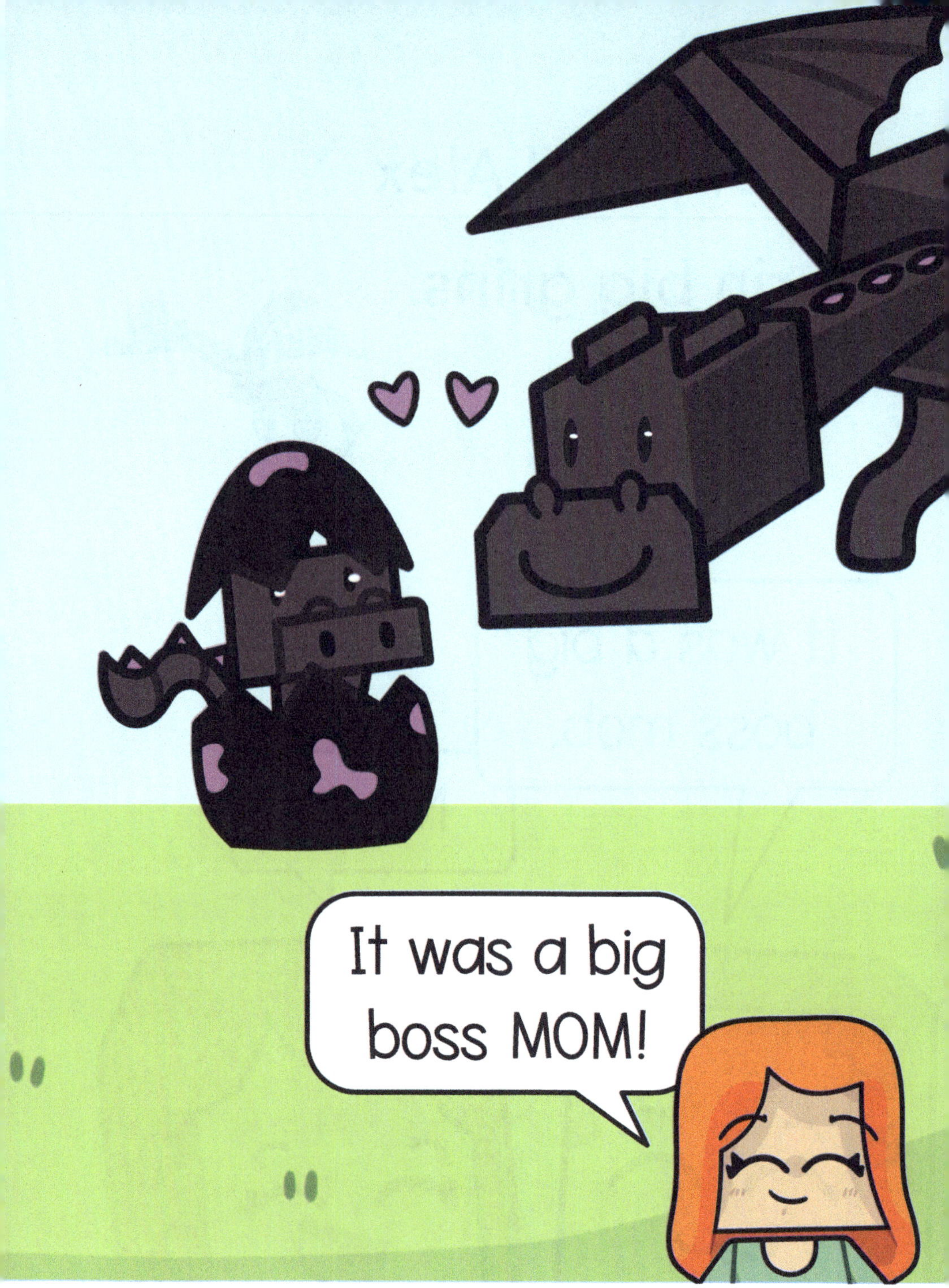

Answer these questions to earn 5XP

1. What were Alex and Steve hunting for? Find the WORD that answers the question.

2. Where did Alex put the egg? Find the SENTENCE that answers the question.

3. Why was the boss mob mad?

4. Why do you think Steve and Alex had different ideas about what to do with the egg?

5. Have you ever given something special to someone else, even though you really wanted to keep it?

You earned 80XP!

Yes!
Let's read Story 4.

Read this story to earn

10XP

Hiss!

Story 4

Read these words to earn

5XP

| slams | drops | catnip | basket |

- have
- they
- come

Ssss...

The mob in this story is a creeper.
Creepers come out at night.
They hiss before they explode, but . . .
creepers are scared of cats!

Phonics Focus: Blends practice

"Cat is not here,"
Alex tells Dog.
"She must be lost!"

Alex and Dog look
for Cat.

They look . . .

and look.

But they do not see her.

Until . . .

"Cat! Come back!"

But Cat will not come back.

"I have a plan to get Cat back," Alex tells Dog.

Alex drops a bit
of catnip in a basket.

She sets the basket
in the grass.
"Here, Cat!" she yells.

Cat sniffs the catnip.
She steps into
the basket.

Alex slams the lid down.

"Got you!"

Alex and Dog set off with Cat in the basket.

They must get back fast.
It is sunset!

Just as dusk sets in,
a mob pops out!

"I have a plan,"
Alex tells Dog.

Alex lifts up the lid of the basket.
Cat pops out.

The mob runs off!

The End

Answer these questions to earn 5XP

1. What did Alex put in the basket? Find the WORD that answers the question.

2. Why did Alex and Dog hurry home? Find the SENTENCE that answers the question.

3. How did Alex catch Cat?

4. Why do you think this story is called "Hiss"?

5. Have you ever had a missing pet? How did you get them back?

You earned 100XP!

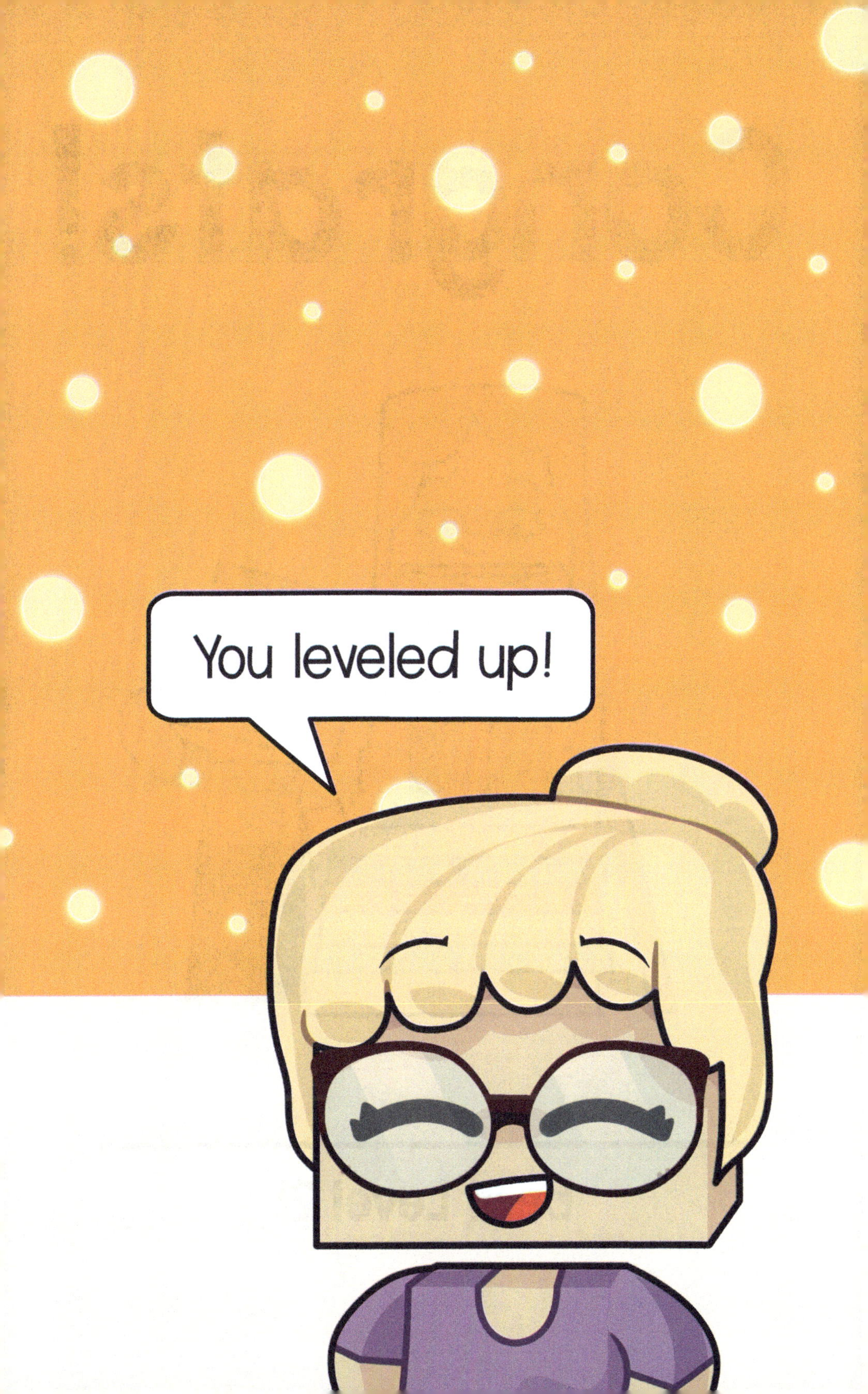
You leveled up!

Congrats!

beat Level 2!

© 2023 Dovetail Readers

Get set for
Level 3
Consonant Digraphs

Available now!

Visit
pixelpagepress.com
for more resources
for Minecraft readers!

Scope and Sequence

Research shows that beginning readers do best when they have explicit, systematic phonics instruction.

The stories in this book start with simple phonics patterns and high frequency words (HFWs), then gradually become more complex.

Here's what your Minecraft reader is practicing in this book:

Level 2
Scope & Sequence

Each story uses the phonics patterns and high frequency words learned in previous stories.

double consonants and -ck

Story 1 HFWs: down, her, look, she

consonant blends, multisyllabic words

Story 2 HFWs: be, for, like

Story 3 HFWs: are, we

Story 4 HFWs: come, have, they

Meet the Creators

Rita Lott is a mom to three little Minecraft fans!

As a literacy specialist, Rita wants kids to be excited about the books they read.

Her favorite Minecraft mobs are Endermen.

Elvis Tapley goes by Simon in real life. He loves drawing and illustrating . . . and playing Minecraft!

His favorite Minecraft mobs are bees.

SCAN TO REVIEW!

Leave Us a Review

★ ★ ★ ★ ★

Did you dig this book?
Leave a review to help more readers discover our books.
Your feedback
keeps us crafters creating!